Mary: Mother of God

By: Shawn Hepburn

"My soul magnifies the Lord.

My spirit has rejoiced in God my Savior,

for he has looked at the humble state of his servant.

For behold, from now on, all generations will call me blessed.

For he who is mighty has done great things for me.

Holy is his name.

His mercy is for generations of generations on those who fear him" (Luke 1:46-50, WEB).

CONTENTS

Introduction

Mary, the mother of Jesus Christ, occupies a unique and profoundly significant place in Christian history. As the woman chosen by God to bring his Son into the world, Mary's life embodies the virtues of faith, humility, and enduring love. Her story resonates with believers across centuries, representing the essence of discipleship and the journey of faith. From her acceptance of the angel Gabriel's message, through her role in Jesus' ministry, and finally to her presence at the crucifixion and beyond, Mary's life is one of extraordinary devotion and strength.

This book aims to explore Mary's life in a way that invites readers to walk alongside her, to witness her joys and sorrows, and to experience her journey of faith in vivid detail. Mary's life is not merely a historical narrative but a spiritual path that calls each believer to seek God with an open heart. Through her story, we can better understand the depth of faith required to embrace divine purpose and to live a life rooted in love and compassion.

Mary's legacy continues to inspire, her memory woven into the prayers, traditions, and hearts of believers across the world. This book will delve into her experiences, her influence on the early church, and her enduring role as a spiritual mother to all who seek to follow Christ. By exploring Mary's life from birth to eternity, we honor her as the mother of the Savior and the mother of faith for generations.

CHAPTER 1: MARY'S EARLY LIFE AND THE ANNUNCIATION

Life in Nazareth

Nestled among the rolling hills of Galilee, the village of Nazareth was a quiet place, its stone houses clustered along dusty pathways that stretched out into fields and olive groves. The rhythm of life in this small community was simple and familiar, shaped by the daily tasks that filled each sunrise and sunset. In this village lived Mary, a young woman known for her gentle nature and her devotion to God. Her days were spent helping her mother prepare meals, gathering water from the village well, and weaving cloth from the wool she helped shear in the spring.

Mary's home was built with thick stone walls that kept the rooms cool in the summer's heat and warm in winter's chill. Inside, the air carried the soft, earthy scent of clay and the warm aroma of freshly baked bread. The simple woven mats on the floor and the sturdy wooden table her father had crafted were testaments to her family's modest means. Their home was small, yet it was filled with peace, the quiet harmony of a family rooted in faith.

As the youngest daughter, Mary had been raised with deep reverence for the sacred words and promises of her people. Her spirit was marked by a quiet strength and unwavering faith, a quality that seemed to radiate from her even in stillness. From a young age, she listened intently to the stories of Israel's history and the ancient promises of the prophets, her heart stirred by the words that spoke of God's faithfulness. She had often heard the words of the prophet Isaiah in the synagogue, words that resonated deeply within her spirit: "Therefore the Lord himself will give you a sign. Behold, the virgin will conceive, and bear a son, and shall call his name Immanuel" (Isaiah 7:14, WEB).

Mary could not have known how these words would come to touch her life in ways she could scarcely imagine. She cherished them, not knowing that the promise of "Immanuel" —"God with us"—would one day shape her path.

The Visit of the Angel Gabriel

One evening, as Mary sat in quiet prayer, she felt a stillness settle around her, deeper than the quiet of night. Suddenly, a radiant light filled the room, casting every corner in a warm, golden glow. Mary's heart quickened as she looked up, startled to see a figure unlike any she had ever encountered. The figure's presence was gentle yet powerful, filling the room with an air of awe and peace. Mary realized she was in the presence of an angel.

The angel spoke, his voice gentle yet resounding, filling the small space with words that seemed to echo in her soul.

"Rejoice, you highly favored one! The Lord is with you. Blessed are you among women" (Luke 1:28, WEB).

Mary felt her heart race, a mixture of confusion and awe filling her spirit. She had never considered herself significant, and the angel's greeting felt beyond her understanding. Why would a messenger of God come to her, a humble girl from Nazareth? She glanced around the room, her eyes seeking something familiar, her mind reeling at the sight before her.

Sensing her unease, the angel's gaze softened, and he spoke again, his words calm and reassuring.

"Don't be afraid, Mary, for you have found favor with God. Behold, you will conceive in your womb, and give birth to a son, and will call his name 'Jesus.' He will be great, and will be called the Son of the Most High. The Lord God will give him the throne of his father, David, and he will reign over the house of Jacob forever. There will be no end to his Kingdom" (Luke 1:30-33, WEB).

Mary listened, her heart filling with awe and a quiet, rising wonder. Yet, a question lingered within her, a simple yet profound question. Gathering her courage, she looked up at the angel, her voice soft but steady.

"How can this be, seeing I am a virgin?" she asked (Luke 1:34, WEB).

The angel's response was filled with mystery, a promise that reached into the very depths of her soul.

"The Holy Spirit will come on you, and the power of the Most High will overshadow you. Therefore also the holy one who is born from you will be called the Son of God. Behold, Elizabeth your relative also has conceived a son in her old age; and this is the sixth month with her who was called barren. For nothing spoken by God is impossible" (Luke 1:35-37, WEB).

Mary felt a quiet calm settle over her, a peace that was both humbling and empowering. Despite the mystery surrounding the angel's words, she knew deep within her heart that God's hand was guiding her. Taking a steady breath, she looked up at the angel, her voice filled with quiet resolve.

"Behold, the servant of the Lord; let it be done to me according to your word" (Luke 1:38, WEB).

The angel's presence began to fade, and as the light dimmed, Mary sat in the stillness of her room, her heart overflowing with a sense of wonder and peace. She placed her hand gently over her heart, feeling the weight of the promise that had been entrusted to her. She was filled with a quiet joy, knowing that her life would be forever changed, set upon a path that only God could have prepared.

The Journey to Elizabeth

In the days that followed, Mary's thoughts returned often to her cousin Elizabeth. The angel had spoken of her, revealing that Elizabeth was already six months pregnant—a miracle, as Elizabeth had been barren for many years. Eager to understand more and to share this journey with someone who might understand, Mary set out on the path to visit Elizabeth. Her heart was filled with a mixture of anticipation, awe, and a need for companionship in this new calling.

The road to Elizabeth's home wound through the hills, dusty and rugged underfoot, but Mary's steps were light, her spirit lifted by the promise she carried. As she walked, she prayed, her hands resting over her heart, feeling a deep connection with God. She found herself contemplating the words of the angel, sensing God's presence close to her as she moved along the familiar paths of the Judean countryside.

When Mary arrived, Elizabeth was already standing at the doorway, her face alight with a radiance that mirrored Mary's own joy. At the sound of Mary's greeting, Elizabeth gasped, her hand resting over her swelling belly. Her eyes filled with tears as she cried out,

"Blessed are you among women, and blessed is the fruit of your womb! Why am I so favored, that the mother of my Lord should come to me? For behold, when the voice of your greeting came into my ears, the baby leaped in my womb for joy! Blessed is she who believed, for there will be a fulfillment of the things which have been spoken to her from the Lord!" (Luke 1:42-45, WEB).

Elizabeth's words washed over Mary like a gentle wave, filling her with confirmation and joy. Her heart felt as if it might overflow, and in that moment, she broke into song, her voice rising in praise, a melody that seemed to echo through the hills.

"My soul magnifies the Lord.
My spirit has rejoiced in God my Savior,
for he has looked at the humble state of his servant.
For behold, from now on, all generations will call me blessed.
For he who is mighty has done great things for me.
Holy is his name.
His mercy is for generations of generations on those who fear him" (Luke 1:46-50, WEB).

Her song, known as the Magnificat, flowed from her heart as a hymn of praise to the God who lifts the humble and fulfills His promises. She sang not only for herself but for all Israel, for every heart that would call her blessed, and for a world about to witness God's promise fulfilled.

Mary stayed with Elizabeth for three months, finding strength and companionship in her cousin's presence. Together, they prayed, sharing their hopes, their fears, and their awe at the unfolding mystery within their lives. In Elizabeth's home, Mary felt a calm assurance, knowing that she was not alone, and that God's promises were already taking shape within her.

Reflection on Mary's Faith

Mary's journey began with a simple "yes." Her obedience, offered without reservation, became the foundation for a life that would bring God's love into the world. Though she could not foresee the fullness of her path, Mary's faith allowed her to embrace the unknown, trusting in the One who had called her.

In Mary's "yes," we find a model of faith and humility, a willingness to let God's purpose unfold in our lives. Her story invites us to say "yes" to God's call, trusting that His plans are greater than we can imagine.

As Mary left Elizabeth's home, her heart was filled with hope and peace, knowing that she was part of something greater than herself. She walked with a steady faith, her spirit lifted by God's promise, and the knowledge that she would never be alone.

Works Cited

The Bible. World English Bible. Public Domain, .

CHAPTER 2: THE JOURNEY TO BETHLEHEM AND THE BIRTH OF JESUS

Setting Out on the Journey to Bethlehem

In those days, a decree went out from Caesar Augustus that all the world should be registered (Luke 2:1, WEB). Even in the quiet hills of Galilee, news of the census reached Nazareth, prompting Joseph to travel to Bethlehem, the city of David, where his lineage lay. Mary, though close to delivering her child, accompanied him, her heart steady with trust that God would be with them.

They left Nazareth at dawn, the air cool and scented with olive trees and wild herbs. Mary rode a gentle donkey, its quiet steps comforting as they left behind the familiar paths of home. Joseph carried provisions—simple cloth bundles filled with bread, dried figs, and olives—and kept a careful pace, casting reassuring glances at Mary. She rested her hands on her growing belly, feeling the presence of her unborn child as a source of both strength and mystery.

The journey to Bethlehem was long and arduous, winding through rocky terrain and narrow, dusty trails. Each day, the sun rose higher, dust settling on their skin and robes. Mary's back ached, but her spirit was unwavering, her heart lifted in quiet prayer as she remembered the angel's words: "He will be great, and will be called the Son of the Most High" (Luke 1:32, WEB). Her strength came from the promises she held within her, and she found peace in the presence of Joseph, whose quiet, steady care reminded her that they were not alone.

At night, they would find shelter under the stars, sometimes resting in olive groves or near the shade of fig trees. Joseph would arrange a soft bed of blankets on the ground, carefully helping Mary down from the donkey, and wrapping her in his cloak to protect her from the night's chill. As they lay beneath the vast, starlit sky, Mary's thoughts turned to her unborn child, her heart swelling with love and anticipation. She whispered prayers to God, trusting that He watched over them, and felt the quiet assurance that she was part of a divine plan.

Arrival in Bethlehem

When they finally reached Bethlehem, dusk had settled over the city. The streets were crowded with travelers, families returning to register for the census, and the city was alive with voices, the clatter of carts, and the scent of smoke rising from hearths. Mary's body was weary, each step carrying a quiet urgency, her breaths growing shallow as she felt the child within her stir.

Joseph, anxious to find a place for Mary to rest, knocked on the doors of several inns. Each innkeeper, seeing the crowds and filled rooms, turned them away, some with apologetic gestures, others with hurried words. Mary watched as Joseph moved from house to house, his determination unwavering as he searched for shelter, his face marked with both concern and resolve.

At last, an innkeeper, seeing Mary's exhaustion, offered them a simple stable at the back of his home. It was humble—a space filled with the warm, earthy scent of hay and the quiet presence of animals—but it was a refuge. Joseph helped Mary settle on a bed of straw, arranging blankets around her to provide warmth. The stable was dimly lit by a single oil lamp, casting gentle shadows on the rough wooden beams and earthen walls, creating a sanctuary of peace amidst the bustling city.

The Birth of Jesus

As night deepened, Mary's labor pains intensified, her body straining with each contraction. She gripped Joseph's hand, finding strength in his presence as he murmured comforting words. She whispered fragments of the psalms she had learned as a child, her heart lifted in prayer: "The Lord is my strength and my shield. My heart has trusted in him, and I am helped" (Psalm 28:7, WEB).

In the stillness of the night, surrounded by the quiet breath of animals and the warmth of straw, Mary brought forth her son. She held him close, marveling at his tiny hands, his soft skin, and the profound stillness that seemed to fill the stable. This was the child of promise, the one foretold by the prophets, the Son of God born not in splendor but in simplicity.

Mary wrapped him carefully in swaddling clothes and laid him in a manger. The soft glow of the lamp bathed his face, and the stable felt transformed, as if heaven itself had drawn close. The peace of the moment was sacred, and Mary felt a joy that surpassed all understanding. The words of Isaiah resonated within her heart: "For to us a child is born, to us a son is given; and the government will be on his shoulders. His name will be called Wonderful Counselor, Mighty God, Everlasting Father, Prince of Peace" (Isaiah 9:6, WEB).

The Visit from the Shepherds

Not long after, the stillness of the stable was broken by the sound of hurried footsteps. Shepherds, clothed in rough garments and bearing the marks of long nights spent in the fields, entered the stable with awe in their eyes. They had come from nearby fields, where they had been watching over their flocks. An angel had appeared to them, surrounded by the glory of the Lord, and they had been filled with fear and wonder.

The shepherds spoke in reverent tones, recounting the angel's message:

"Don't be afraid, for behold, I bring you good news of great joy which will be to all the people. For there is born to you today, in David's city, a Savior, who is Christ the Lord" (Luke 2:10-11, WEB).

The shepherds knelt before the manger, their faces reflecting the light of the lamp as they gazed upon the newborn child. Mary watched them, her heart swelling with joy and gratitude, knowing that this birth was not only for her but for all of Israel, and beyond. These humble shepherds were the first to witness the Messiah, chosen by God to bear witness to this holy night. Mary felt a deep sense of connection with them, sharing in their humility and reverence.

"But Mary kept all these sayings, pondering them in her heart" (Luke 2:19, WEB).

Miraculous Signs and Gnostic Accounts of Wonder

According to the Protoevangelium of James and The Gospel of Pseudo-Matthew, this night was marked by signs and wonders, both within the stable and beyond its walls. The Protoevangelium of James recounts that at the moment of Jesus' birth, time itself seemed to pause. The world held its breath, as if all of creation recognized the significance of the event. People in nearby houses stopped in their tracks, animals ceased their sounds, and an unearthly peace fell over the land.

In The Gospel of Pseudo-Matthew, it is written that a great light filled the stable at the moment of Jesus' birth, a light so pure and radiant that it banished the shadows, illuminating every corner of the humble space. The animals in the stable, sensing the sacredness of the event, knelt in quiet reverence, their breaths still as they bore witness to the arrival of the divine.

Mary observed these signs with awe, sensing that her son's arrival was not only a fulfillment of prophecy but also a cosmic event that resonated across the heavens and earth. She held him close, feeling the warmth of his small body against her, and she prayed that she might have the strength to guide him in the life that awaited.

Reflection on Mary's Faith and Joseph's Devotion

As the night wore on, Mary and Joseph shared a moment of silent wonder. Joseph's heart was filled with gratitude and awe, his role as protector and father settling deeply within him. He watched Mary as she cradled Jesus, feeling both humbled and honored to be part of God's plan.

For Mary, the journey of faith had only begun. She had trusted in God's word and had carried His promise to fruition, yet she sensed the weight of her calling with each passing moment. She understood that her role as the mother of the Messiah was one that would bring both joy and sorrow, blessings and challenges. But in that sacred night, holding her son close, she felt a profound peace, trusting that God would guide her path.

Together, Mary and Joseph offered a prayer of thanksgiving, asking for God's guidance as they stepped into the unknown. As they drifted into a quiet rest, the stable around them seemed to glow with a quiet holiness, as if all of creation had come to bear witness to the miracle that had unfolded.

Works Cited

The Bible. World English Bible. Public Domain, .

Protoevangelium of James. In The Apocryphal New Testament, translated by J. K. Elliott, Oxford University Press, 1993.

Gospel of Pseudo-Matthew. In The Other Gospels: Accounts of Jesus from Outside the New Testament, edited by Bart D. Ehrman and Zlatko Pleše, Oxford University Press, 2014.

CHAPTER 3: MARY'S EARLY YEARS WITH JESUS

Life in Nazareth and Mary's Role as a Mother

In the quiet village of Nazareth, life was simple yet rich with the rhythms of family and faith. Mary and Joseph's home was small, nestled among olive trees and stone pathways where village life unfolded each day. The air carried the scent of earth and olive oil, mingling with the warmth of freshly baked bread and the sounds of children playing nearby.

Mary spent her days guiding her family in faith and love, ensuring her children grew up with a deep reverence for God. Jesus, her firstborn, seemed to carry a quiet wisdom even as a young child. Mary observed his gentleness, his curiosity about the world, and his remarkable attentiveness during times of prayer. She sensed within him the presence of God's Spirit, a mystery she pondered in her heart.

Mary's teachings were simple yet profound. She taught her children the prayers of their ancestors and recounted stories of God's promises to Israel. She would gather Jesus and his siblings, including young James, and tell them of the prophets who spoke of the coming Messiah. In her heart, Mary knew Jesus was destined to fulfill these promises, yet she raised him with humility, teaching him to honor the ways of their people and to cherish those around him.

The Presentation in the Temple and the Prophecies of Simeon and Anna

When Jesus was an infant, Mary and Joseph brought him to the Temple in Jerusalem to fulfill the purification rites as commanded by the Law of Moses (Luke 2:22, WEB). The journey was a solemn one, filled with reverence as they approached the magnificent stone structure that rose above the city. The Temple courts bustled with the sounds of pilgrims, the scent of incense, and the murmured prayers of worshippers. Mary felt a sacred awe as she carried Jesus into the Temple, her heart lifted in silent prayer.

In the Temple, they met Simeon, a righteous man who had awaited the coming of the Messiah with unshakable faith. The Holy Spirit had promised him he would not see death before he had seen the Lord's Christ. As soon as Simeon saw Jesus, he took the child in his arms, his face filled with joy and reverence, and blessed God:

"Now you are releasing your servant, Master, according to your word, in peace; for my eyes have seen your salvation, which you have prepared before the face of all peoples; a light for revelation to the nations, and the glory of your people Israel" (Luke 2:29-32, WEB).

Mary listened, her heart swelling with wonder at Simeon's words. She felt the weight of her role as Jesus' mother, a mixture of honor and trepidation. Turning to her, Simeon offered a somber prophecy: "Behold, this child is set for the falling and the rising of many in Israel, and for a sign which is spoken against. Yes, a sword will pierce through your own soul, that the thoughts of many hearts may be revealed" (Luke 2:34-35, WEB).

Nearby, Anna, an elderly prophetess who had spent years in prayer and fasting within the Temple, approached them. Her face lit up when she saw Jesus, and she began to give thanks to God, speaking of the redemption he would bring to all Jerusalem. Mary watched Anna's joy with gratitude, knowing that these moments would strengthen her faith in the years to come.

The words of Simeon and Anna stayed with Mary as they returned to Nazareth, forming a quiet but enduring part of her prayers. She pondered the mysteries surrounding her son, sensing the deep and powerful purpose within him and accepting that her journey would be one of both joy and sorrow.

Miraculous Moments from Jesus' Childhood

As Jesus grew, there were moments when his unique nature shone through the simplicity of daily life, filling Mary with awe and reverence. According to the Protoevangelium of James, Mary had always sensed God's hand upon Jesus, even from his earliest days. His kindness and calmness as a young child often left others around him in wonder, and she could see that his heart was attuned to something far greater than himself.

In the Gospel of Pseudo-Matthew, it is recounted that one day while Jesus was playing with other children near a stream, he shaped twelve small birds out of clay. While the other children watched in amazement, he clapped his hands, and the birds took flight, alive and fluttering into the sky. The children were delighted, but others looked on in awe, unable to explain this miraculous sight. Mary observed these wonders with a mother's love and caution, understanding that her son carried a gift that was both beautiful and divine. She gently guided Jesus, teaching him humility and kindness, helping him understand that his abilities were not for self-gain but to reveal God's goodness.

In another instance, according to Pseudo-Matthew, Mary saw Jesus perform a small miracle of healing. A neighbor's son had fallen gravely ill, and when Jesus came to his bedside, he placed his small hand over the boy's forehead. The fever lifted, and the boy awoke, his strength restored. The neighbors marveled at Jesus' power, and though Mary shared in their awe, she reminded Jesus of the responsibility that came with such gifts.

Mary's love for her son grew with each passing day, her faith deepening as she observed the glimpses of his calling. She prayed that God would grant her the wisdom to guide him, nurturing his heart and helping him understand that his power was part of a greater plan. These early years were filled with moments of beauty and mystery, each one weaving together a deeper understanding of her role as his mother.

A Time of Refuge in Egypt and Jesus' Early Signs of Divinity

During the family's time in Egypt, stories of Jesus' miraculous nature continued to spread. As recounted in Pseudo-Matthew, Mary and Joseph, seeking safety from King Herod's decree, found refuge among kind strangers and in humble homes. Even in these foreign lands, Jesus' presence seemed to carry peace and healing. One day, Mary encountered a young child who had fallen ill. With her encouragement, Jesus laid his small hands on the child, and the illness lifted, leaving the child restored and healthy. Those who witnessed these acts were filled with awe, recognizing the divine presence within the child.

Mary sensed that her journey with Jesus would continue to unfold in mysterious ways. She relied on her faith as she navigated these challenges, finding strength in the bond they shared. Joseph was her steadfast companion in this time of exile, his faith unwavering as he protected and cared for Mary and Jesus.

In another instance, the Protoevangelium of James describes how, even as an infant, Jesus seemed to have a calming effect on animals and people alike. In Egypt, they were offered shelter by a family with livestock, and when Jesus entered, the animals turned their faces toward him, kneeling as if recognizing the holiness of the child. Mary watched with a mixture of awe and humility, realizing that even creation bore witness to her son's presence.

Mary's Role in Teaching and Mentoring Her Children

Upon their return to Nazareth, Mary resumed the routines of village life, raising Jesus alongside his siblings, including James, who looked up to his older brother with admiration. Mary guided her children with love, teaching them to respect others, care for the poor, and find strength in God's word. She encouraged Jesus' natural compassion, watching as he treated each person with dignity and love, even at a young age.

James, too, grew under Mary's nurturing care. Though he would later come to question Jesus' mission, in his early years, he learned the same lessons of faith and humility that Mary instilled in each of her children. Mary sensed that her family was part of God's unfolding plan, and she prayed that each of her children would find their role within it. Her love and guidance shaped their lives, preparing them for the journey ahead, and her teachings became a foundation that would remain with them.

Reflection on Mary's Faith and Wisdom as a Mother

Mary's early years with Jesus were filled with moments of beauty, wonder, and quiet faith. She had been entrusted with raising the Son of God, a responsibility that filled her with both joy and awe. Each day, she sought to instill in him the values of humility, kindness, and reverence, sensing that her role as his mother was both sacred and transformative.

In these tender years, Mary's faith grew deeper as she witnessed the early signs of Jesus' calling. She found strength in God's promise, drawing upon her quiet faith and inner wisdom to guide him. Her life was a testament to obedience, humility, and a love that endured both the ordinary and the miraculous. In Mary's example, we see the essence of faith—a heart open to God's call, trusting in His purpose even when the path remains hidden.

Works Cited

The Bible. World English Bible. Public Domain, .

Protoevangelium of James. In The Apocryphal New Testament, translated by J. K. Elliott, Oxford University Press, 1993.

Gospel of Pseudo-Matthew. In The Other Gospels: Accounts of Jesus from Outside the New Testament, edited by Bart D. Ehrman and Zlatko Pleše, Oxford University Press, 2014.

CHAPTER 4: JESUS IN THE TEMPLE AND MARY'S ROLE IN HIS GROWTH

The Journey to Jerusalem and the Festival of Passover

As Jesus grew, so did his wisdom and understanding. Each year, Mary and Joseph made the journey to Jerusalem to celebrate the Feast of Passover, following the tradition commanded in the Law of Moses. This annual pilgrimage was a significant event for Jewish families, a time to honor God's deliverance and renew their covenant with Him. For Mary, the journey had an added meaning—she observed Jesus' awe and reverence as he learned about the heritage of his people. With each passing year, she saw in him a deepening awareness of his faith and purpose, something that filled her heart with both pride and reverence.

The roads leading to Jerusalem were alive with pilgrims from distant towns and villages, their voices mingling with the sounds of livestock and the clatter of carts. Mary held Jesus' hand as they walked, guiding him through the throngs of people, and pointing out the sights and sounds that marked this sacred journey. She could feel his excitement, his eyes wide with wonder as they

MARY: MOTHER OF GOD

neared the holy city, its magnificent temple standing tall above the rooftops.

In the Temple courts, the air was thick with the scent of incense and the sounds of prayers and offerings. Mary felt a sense of peace as she entered, knowing she was part of a tradition that stretched back through generations. This was a place of devotion, where God's presence felt especially near, and she felt her heart lifted in praise and gratitude.

The Lost and Found Messiah

As they celebrated the Feast of Passover, Mary and Joseph were busy attending to the rituals and requirements of the festival. The Temple was filled with worshippers, and the atmosphere was a mixture of reverence and joy. When the festival ended, they began the journey home, traveling with a large group of relatives and friends. They assumed that Jesus was with the other children, moving freely among the crowd.

However, as they paused for the evening, Mary felt an unease creeping into her heart. She searched the gathering for Jesus, expecting to find him among his cousins, but as the moments passed and he remained absent, her worry grew. Joseph shared her concern, and together they retraced their steps, asking everyone in their group if they had seen Jesus. Realizing that he was not with them, Mary's heart raced with fear.

They returned to Jerusalem, their minds filled with anxious thoughts, searching for three days. Mary's heart ached with each passing hour, her prayers rising in desperate hope that they would find him safe. She thought of the angel's promise and the many signs she had witnessed in his young life, yet at this moment, she felt the full weight of her responsibility as his mother. Her heart was filled with both a mother's fear and a deep reverence, understanding that Jesus was not only her child but a child entrusted to her by God.

At last, they found Jesus in the Temple, seated among the teachers, listening to them and asking questions. His face was serene, his eyes bright with understanding, and he seemed entirely absorbed in the conversation. The teachers were astonished at his answers, marveling at the wisdom that flowed from someone so young.

Seeing him there, Mary felt a rush of relief and wonder, her heart torn between joy and frustration. She approached him, her voice filled with a mother's love and worry:

"Son, why have you treated us this way? Behold, your father and I were anxiously looking for you" (Luke 2:48, WEB).

Jesus looked up at her, his expression calm and filled with a quiet understanding that seemed beyond his years.

"Why were you looking for me? Didn't you know that I must be in my Father's house?" he replied (Luke 2:49, WEB).

Mary held his gaze, her heart filled with a mixture of awe and humility. She did not fully understand his words, but she knew they held a truth that went beyond her own comprehension. Quietly, she accepted the mystery of her son's calling, a calling that would unfold in ways she could scarcely imagine.

"And he went down with them, and came to Nazareth. He was subject to them, and his mother kept all these sayings in her heart" (Luke 2:51, WEB).

Jesus' Development and Mary's Role as His Guide

As Jesus returned with Mary and Joseph to Nazareth, his life resumed its simple rhythms. Yet, moments like those in the Temple reminded Mary of the depth within her son, a depth that would one day reveal itself to the world. She observed his growth with a mother's quiet pride and a sense of reverence for the divine purpose that lay within him.

Mary continued to guide him with love and wisdom, drawing

upon the stories of their ancestors and the teachings of God's law. She taught him humility and compassion, emphasizing the importance of kindness to strangers, generosity to the poor, and gratitude to God for all things. According to the Protoevangelium of James, Mary had been set apart from her own birth, her life marked by purity and devotion. She brought these qualities into her role as a mother, creating a home filled with faith and the love of God.

Mary's teachings went beyond words; they were reflected in her actions, in the care with which she performed each task, and in her steadfast faith. She showed Jesus and his siblings the importance of patience, forgiveness, and understanding. Her love became a foundation upon which Jesus would build his own ministry, shaping his view of the world and his relationship with God.

In moments of stillness, Mary would often reflect on the prophecies she had heard as a child, and the promises spoken over her son. She sensed the depth of his calling, and though she could not fully understand it, she trusted in God's wisdom. She prayed daily, asking for guidance, for the strength to fulfill her role, and for Jesus to grow into the man God had destined him to become.

Miraculous Signs and Wonder from Apocryphal Sources

In addition to the biblical accounts, the Gospel of Pseudo-Matthew offers glimpses of miraculous moments during Jesus' youth that filled Mary with awe and a deepened sense of his divine nature. In one instance, Jesus was said to have performed a small miracle by lengthening a piece of wood for Joseph while he worked in his carpentry shop. Joseph had been distressed that the wood was too short for the task, but when Jesus touched it, the wood stretched to the required length. Witnessing this, Mary saw in her son a power that was gentle yet undeniably divine, and she continued to guide him with humility, knowing that his gifts were meant for a greater purpose.

According to the Protoevangelium of James, people around Nazareth began to notice unusual occurrences wherever Jesus was present. When he passed by a withered tree, it would sometimes spring to life, its leaves unfurling in his presence as if responding to the source of life within him. Such signs brought wonder to those who witnessed them, and though Mary marveled at these glimpses of his power, she reminded Jesus of the importance of humility and kindness, guiding him to use his gifts wisely and for the glory of God.

Mary's Faith in the Mystery of Jesus' Calling

As Jesus grew, Mary continued to observe his journey with both love and reverence, nurturing his heart while honoring the divine mystery within him. She knew that her son was not only hers but belonged to God, and she trusted in God's plan, even as she felt the weight of Simeon's prophecy that a sword would pierce her soul. Her prayers became the bedrock of her strength, and she remained a steadfast source of guidance, encouragement, and unwavering faith for Jesus.

Through these early years, Mary's life was a testament to patience, humility, and quiet wisdom. She was a mother chosen not only to nurture the Son of God but to be his first teacher, his first example of love and devotion. She carried the words of the angel, the blessings of Simeon and Anna, and the mysteries of her son's childhood miracles within her heart, accepting the unknowns and trusting in the God who had chosen her for this sacred path.

In Mary's journey, we find a profound example of faith—a faith that embraces both the known and the unknowable, that endures through moments of wonder and moments of fear. Her life reminds us that true faith is not only about understanding but about trusting, even when the path remains hidden. In Mary, we see the heart of a mother whose love and faith shaped the Son of God, preparing him for the path he would one day walk.

Works Cited

The Bible. World English Bible. Public Domain, .

Protoevangelium of James. In The Apocryphal New Testament, translated by J. K. Elliott, Oxford University Press, 1993.

Gospel of Pseudo-Matthew. In The Other Gospels: Accounts of Jesus from Outside the New Testament, edited by Bart D. Ehrman and Zlatko Pleše, Oxford University Press, 2014.

CHAPTER 5: MARY'S ROLE IN JESUS' MINISTRY AND THE WEDDING AT CANA

Mary's Transition from Mother to Follower

As Jesus grew into adulthood, Mary felt a deepening awareness that her role in his life was evolving. For years, she had been his mother and his first teacher, guiding him in the ways of faith and wisdom. But as Jesus neared the beginning of his ministry, Mary sensed a shift. She saw him increasingly absorbed in prayer and contemplation, his gaze often lingering on the distant hills, as if awaiting a call that only he could hear.

Mary had carried the promise of his calling within her heart since the angel Gabriel's visit, but as that promise unfolded, she felt both pride and humility. She realized that Jesus was no longer simply her son but was now becoming the teacher, healer, and Messiah that Simeon had prophesied he would be. While the Protoevangelium of James had described Mary as a woman set apart from her own birth, her life marked by purity and devotion, now she saw that Jesus too was stepping into his own sacred destiny.

In quiet moments of prayer, Mary asked for the strength to let go, to allow Jesus the space he needed to fulfill God's plan. Her faith was deep, and though she did not fully understand all that would come, she trusted that God's purpose would be revealed in time.

The Wedding at Cana: Mary's Faith in Jesus' Power

Mary's faith in her son was soon put to the test. She and Jesus, along with his disciples, attended a wedding in Cana, a small village not far from Nazareth. The celebration was joyous, the air filled with laughter, music, and the clinking of glasses as friends and family gathered to celebrate. Mary enjoyed the warmth of the gathering, watching Jesus as he conversed with the other guests, his presence calm and comforting.

During the festivities, Mary noticed a quiet commotion among the servants. She learned that the wine had run out—a potential embarrassment for the host and an issue that could dampen the joy of the occasion. Feeling a quiet nudge in her heart, she approached Jesus, her voice soft but confident, "They have no wine" (John 2:3, WEB).

Jesus looked at her, his expression filled with gentle understanding. He knew she believed in him, that she sensed he could help, though he replied, "Woman, what does that have to do with you and me? My hour has not yet come" (John 2:4, WEB). The words might have seemed dismissive, yet Mary's faith was unwavering. She simply turned to the servants, instructing them, "Whatever he says to you, do it" (John 2:5, WEB).

Jesus, seeing the trust in his mother's eyes and the need of those around him, responded with compassion. He instructed the servants to fill six stone water jars with water. When they drew the liquid from the jars, they found it had turned into wine—wine of a quality so fine that the guests marveled at its taste. This miracle marked the beginning of Jesus' ministry, a sign of his divine nature revealed, and Mary felt both awe and gratitude, witnessing the promise she had cherished for so long come to life before her.

Mary's Steadfast Support in Jesus' Ministry

Following the wedding at Cana, Jesus began his public ministry, traveling from village to village, preaching the kingdom of God, healing the sick, and performing miracles. Mary understood that her son's path had now led him far beyond the walls of their home in Nazareth, and though her heart missed him, she supported him fully. She recognized that his calling would transform lives, not just in Galilee, but throughout Israel and beyond.

According to the Gospel of Pseudo-Matthew, Mary was not only Jesus' mother but his first follower, witnessing his teachings and works with unwavering faith. She followed Jesus to many of the towns he visited, watching as he healed the sick, gave sight to the blind, and proclaimed God's love to all who would listen. Mary saw how his words touched people's hearts, how his compassion lifted the weary, and how his presence brought hope to those who had lived in despair.

In one instance, Jesus healed a leper in Mary's presence, touching the man's face, his hand steady as he spoke words of healing. Mary felt a rush of joy and reverence, recognizing in her son's actions the fulfillment of God's promise. She carried these moments within her heart, each one a testament to the depth of Jesus' love and his calling to restore humanity.

Mary's Faith in the Face of Growing Resistance

As Jesus' ministry grew, so did the opposition from religious authorities and others who questioned his teachings. Rumors and criticisms followed him, and Mary, hearing of these challenges, felt the weight of concern. She knew that following God's path was rarely without struggle, but seeing her son criticized and misunderstood was a pain that pierced her deeply.

Mary, however, never wavered. She prayed for him daily, her faith serving as both her strength and her solace. She remembered the words of Simeon, spoken so long ago in the Temple: "Yes, a sword will pierce through your own soul" (Luke 2:35, WEB). In moments of solitude, she reflected on these words, sensing that her journey with Jesus would require both courage and faith.

Despite the growing resistance, Mary continued to support Jesus, trusting in God's plan. She understood that his mission would not be easy, and she carried each challenge with a heart anchored in prayer. Her faith was steadfast, her love unwavering, and her commitment to God's purpose unbreakable.

Mary's Place in the Early Community of Followers

As Jesus' teachings spread, Mary's role within his circle of followers became one of quiet guidance and support. She nurtured a close bond with the other disciples, many of whom regarded her as a motherly figure, a source of wisdom and comfort. She shared stories of Jesus' early life with them, encouraging them to remain faithful and strong in their mission.

Mary's humility and kindness drew others to her, and her presence became a stabilizing force within the early Christian community. According to the Gospel of Pseudo-Matthew, her life was one of unwavering devotion, a reflection of her faith and the strength she had cultivated throughout her years of walking with God. She continued to support Jesus in every way she could, offering encouragement to the disciples and strengthening them in their resolve to follow his teachings.

When doubts arose, Mary reminded them of Jesus' miracles, his compassion, and the love that marked his every action. She understood that each of them was chosen for this purpose, and she felt a profound gratitude that she was part of something so much greater than herself.

Reflection on Mary's Faith and Her Role as the First Believer

Mary's journey from Nazareth to Cana and into the heart of Jesus' ministry was a journey of faith, one that revealed her transformation from mother to follower, from teacher to disciple. She had borne him as a child, raised him in faith, and now supported him as he revealed the kingdom of God to the world.

In Mary's unwavering support, we see the essence of true faith —a willingness to follow God's call, even when the path is uncertain. Her life was a testament to devotion, courage, and humility, qualities that shaped not only her son but also the early community of believers who would one day carry his teachings to the world.

Her presence at the wedding in Cana, her quiet encouragement in the face of challenges, and her steadfast love became the foundation of the Church's faith. In Mary, we see the first believer, the one who carried the promise and shared in the fulfillment. Her journey is a profound example of faith, love, and the power of God's purpose unfolding through a life lived in humble obedience.

Works Cited

The Bible. World English Bible. Public Domain, .

Protoevangelium of James. In The Apocryphal New Testament, translated by J. K. Elliott, Oxford University Press, 1993.

Gospel of Pseudo-Matthew. In The Other Gospels: Accounts of Jesus from Outside the New Testament, edited by Bart D. Ehrman and Zlatko Pleše, Oxford University Press, 2014.

CHAPTER 6: MARY'S PRESENCE THROUGH JESUS' MINISTRY AND THE CROSS

Mary's Growing Role Among the Disciples

As Jesus' ministry grew, Mary found herself increasingly woven into the lives of his followers. She was a source of stability and encouragement, her faith a quiet example to those who followed Jesus. The disciples came to regard her as a spiritual mother, seeking her guidance, comfort, and insight during moments of doubt and difficulty. In the Gospel of Mary, Mary Magdalene is often depicted as a close companion of Jesus, and this gospel reveals the profound respect the other disciples had for women in their community. Mary, Jesus' mother, shared in this respect and became a nurturing figure for the early followers, providing both wisdom and maternal support.

Mary would often reflect on the teachings of her son, pondering the ways in which his words connected to the ancient promises of God. She felt an unspoken kinship with Mary Magdalene and other women disciples, united in their commitment to Jesus' message and mission. The women in Jesus' ministry, including Joanna and Susanna, looked to her as a guiding presence. These women formed a close bond, their hearts united by faith and strengthened by Mary's quiet resolve.

Witnessing the Miracles and the Power of Faith

Throughout Jesus' ministry, Mary observed miracles that affirmed her faith and the divine calling of her son. She watched as he healed the blind, cleansed lepers, and fed the hungry, each act a reflection of God's love and mercy. The Gospel of Pseudo-Matthew recounts moments when Jesus' power and compassion moved even the hardest hearts, leaving his followers awestruck. Mary was deeply moved by each miracle, her heart overflowing with gratitude as she saw God's hand in every act of healing and grace.

One day, while following Jesus through a crowded village, Mary witnessed a man who had been paralyzed for many years approach Jesus with the help of friends. With a touch and a few words, Jesus restored the man's mobility, and Mary felt a wave of awe wash over her as the crowd marveled at this miracle. In such moments, she could feel the truth of God's promise to Israel fulfilled in her son, and her heart was filled with a sense of purpose and reverence.

Mary's presence was an anchor for others who had experienced Jesus' miracles. As she interacted with those whose lives were changed by his touch, she reminded them to hold their faith steadfastly, knowing that each act was a testament to God's love and power. Her voice was gentle but sure, her words uplifting as she spoke of the God who loved and healed through her son.

Mary's Faith Amidst Growing Opposition and Her Role as a Pillar of Strength

As Jesus' popularity grew, so did the opposition he faced. The religious leaders and authorities felt threatened by his teachings, and the tension around him began to escalate. Rumors and accusations circulated, and Mary's heart grew heavy as she sensed the impending trials her son would face. The Protoevangelium of James hints at Mary's deep-rooted strength and faith, qualities she relied on as she watched the mounting resistance against her son.

Mary knew that Jesus' ministry was bound to disrupt the established order, but she also understood the risks involved. The words Simeon had spoken years ago in the Temple—"A sword will pierce through your own soul" (Luke 2:35, WEB)—echoed in her mind. She prayed fervently, seeking God's strength and wisdom to support Jesus and the disciples, especially as hostility grew.

Mary's quiet presence became a source of comfort for Jesus and his followers. She continued to offer words of encouragement, her faith unshaken even in the face of uncertainty. She reminded the disciples of Jesus' teachings, his words of hope and love, and the promise that God's light would overcome all darkness. Her faith was a refuge, a reminder that no matter the cost, their journey was held in God's hands.

At the Cross: Mary's Suffering and Her Faith in God's Promise

As Jesus' mission brought him to Jerusalem for the Passover, Mary felt a deep foreboding in her heart. She had journeyed with him every step of the way, and now, as she walked through the city's streets filled with tension, she sensed that his path was nearing its end. The Gospel of John recounts how, during Jesus' trial and crucifixion, Mary stood at the foot of the cross, her heart breaking as she watched her son suffer.

The Roman soldiers nailed Jesus to the cross, his body pierced and bruised, and Mary's pain was unimaginable. She felt Simeon's prophecy come true—a sword had indeed pierced her soul. Yet, even in her anguish, she stood firm, her eyes locked on her son, her presence a silent testament to her love and faith.

"When Jesus therefore saw his mother, and the disciple whom he loved standing there, he said to his mother, 'Woman, behold, your son!' Then he said to the disciple, 'Behold, your mother!' From that hour, the disciple took her to his own home" (John 19:26-27, WEB).

In that moment, Mary's heart was both shattered and strengthened. She understood that her role was not yet complete. Jesus had entrusted her to John, and by doing so, he extended her role as a mother to encompass his followers, uniting her with them in their grief and in their faith. In her son's final moments, he gave her a new family, binding her to the early Christian community in a sacred act of love.

The Gospel of Mary, a Gnostic text, describes Mary Magdalene's vision and encouragement to the disciples following Jesus' death, affirming that women played a pivotal role in the early Christian movement. Mary, too, embodied this strength, supporting and encouraging the disciples with a resolve born from her own faith and the knowledge that her son's mission had only begun.

After the Crucifixion: Mary's Role Among the Early Followers

In the days following Jesus' crucifixion, Mary remained with the disciples, grieving her son's death while also comforting those around her. Her sorrow was deep, but her faith was unwavering. According to The Gospel of Pseudo-Matthew, Mary was revered by the disciples, who looked to her as both a mother and a spiritual guide. Her presence was a reminder of Jesus' love, a living testament to his teachings.

When news of the resurrection reached them, Mary's sorrow turned to joy, her faith rewarded by the promise of eternal life fulfilled. Though she had endured unimaginable pain, she now felt the triumph of God's plan, knowing that Jesus had conquered death. She became a witness to the resurrection, a beacon of hope for those who doubted, assuring them that God's promises were true.

Mary continued to support the disciples as they spread Jesus' teachings, her role shifting from mother to matriarch of the early Church. Her faith and endurance inspired those around her, particularly the women disciples, who followed her example of strength and devotion. Mary's life was a profound witness to God's love, her journey a testament to faith that had persevered through both joy and suffering.

Reflection on Mary's Enduring Faith

Mary's journey with Jesus—from Nazareth to the cross, and finally to the resurrection—was one of faith, love, and unwavering devotion. She had been the first to believe, the first to say "yes" to God's plan, and in her quiet strength, she became the foundation of the early Christian community. Her presence among the disciples was a source of comfort and courage, her faith a guiding light in the uncertain days that followed Jesus' death.

In Mary, we see the epitome of faith—a heart that embraced both the joys and sorrows of God's calling, a life that reflected obedience, humility, and love. She walked the path God had set before her, bearing both the miraculous and the painful with grace. Her life remains an example for all who seek to follow God with an open heart, trusting in His promises even when the path is difficult.

Mary's legacy lives on, her faith a source of strength for all who seek God's presence in their lives. She is a mother to the Church, a reminder that faith endures through all trials, and a testament to the power of love that transcends even death.

Works Cited

The Bible. World English Bible. Public Domain, .

Protoevangelium of James. In The Apocryphal New Testament, translated by J. K. Elliott, Oxford University Press, 1993.

Gospel of Pseudo-Matthew. In The Other Gospels: Accounts of Jesus from Outside the New Testament, edited by Bart D. Ehrman and Zlatko Pleše, Oxford University Press, 2014.

Gospel of Mary. In The Nag Hammadi Scriptures, edited by Marvin Meyer, HarperOne, 2007.

CHAPTER 7: MARY'S ROLE IN THE EARLY CHURCH AND HER LEGACY

Mary's Presence Among the Disciples After the Resurrection

After the resurrection, Mary's life took on new significance within the early Christian community. She remained a steadfast presence among the disciples, supporting them through times of uncertainty and change. Her faith, strengthened through years of following Jesus, became an anchor for those who struggled with doubts and fears. The Gospel of Mary portrays her as a central figure, deeply respected by Jesus' followers, including Peter and Mary Magdalene, who sought her guidance in interpreting Jesus' teachings.

The days following Jesus' resurrection were filled with joy and wonder, yet they were also marked by questions and concerns about the future of their mission. In this new era, Mary became not only a mother to Jesus' followers but also a guiding voice of wisdom and hope. She comforted them with stories of Jesus' early life, sharing the moments of love, faith, and miracles that had defined their journey together. Her memories of Jesus strengthened the disciples, helping them hold onto his message as they prepared to spread his teachings across distant lands.

Mary's Role in the Formation of the Early Church

As the early Church began to take shape, Mary played an essential role, though she remained humble and often unseen by the world. She was present at gatherings of believers, sharing in their prayers and guiding their understanding of Jesus' teachings. The disciples held her in deep reverence, seeing in her both the wisdom of a mother and the strength of a true disciple. In the Gospel of Pseudo-Matthew, Mary is portrayed as a figure of unwavering devotion, embodying the values of love, humility, and faithfulness that Jesus had taught.

Mary's presence offered the disciples a sense of continuity with Jesus, grounding them in the knowledge that God's love was constant and unchanging. She reminded them that Jesus had called them to serve, to love, and to forgive. Her life became a model of discipleship, demonstrating that faithfulness meant not only following Jesus in times of joy but also in moments of sorrow and sacrifice.

Mary was a voice of encouragement as the apostles went forth to preach, reminding them to rely on God's strength. Her words and actions carried the echoes of Jesus' teachings, and her influence was felt in every corner of the early Christian community. She stood alongside the women disciples, such as Mary Magdalene, Joanna, and Susanna, empowering them to share the good news and serve others with compassion and courage.

Mary's Final Years and Her Devotion to Prayer

In her later years, Mary's life was devoted to prayer and quiet service. She spent her days in reflection, often praying for the safety and courage of the apostles who were spreading Jesus' message far and wide. According to tradition, she lived with the Apostle John, whom Jesus had entrusted her to from the cross, and she found comfort in his presence, as he reminded her of the times they had shared with Jesus.

Mary's prayers were filled with gratitude, her spirit lifted by the knowledge that Jesus' mission was being fulfilled. She prayed for those who faced persecution, lifting them up in her heart and trusting that God's love would sustain them. Her presence became a source of peace for those around her, as she reminded them that their trials were part of a greater plan. Her faith was a quiet, unbreakable force, reflecting the love she had carried since the day the angel had appeared to her.

In her moments of reflection, Mary would often recall her journey with Jesus—the miracle of his birth, the days of his childhood, and the miracles and teachings that had shaped his ministry. Her life was a prayer, a continuous offering to God in honor of the son she had loved and the Savior she had believed in with all her heart.

The Assumption of Mary: Tradition and Belief

Though the New Testament does not recount Mary's passing, Christian tradition holds that she was assumed body and soul into heaven. This belief, celebrated by the Church as the Assumption, reflects the reverence held for Mary and the understanding of her unique role in salvation history. According to apocryphal sources and early Church teachings, Mary's passing was not marked by the ordinary sorrow of death, but rather by a peaceful transition to eternal life, her earthly journey completed in God's presence.

The Protoevangelium of James suggests that Mary was set apart from birth, chosen by God to bear the Savior, and her Assumption is seen as the completion of this divine plan. As she was lifted into heaven, it is believed that she was reunited with her son, who welcomed her into the eternal kingdom she had so faithfully believed in.

This belief in Mary's Assumption holds that, even in death, she did not experience the decay of the body, as she was preserved from the effects of sin. Her life had been marked by purity, faith, and an unbroken bond with God. The Assumption honors her as the first disciple, the mother of the Church, and a symbol of hope for all believers who seek God's presence in their own lives.

Mary's Legacy and Her Role as a Model of Faith

Mary's life, from the quiet village of Nazareth to the crucifixion and beyond, remains a testament to faith, obedience, and love. She is remembered as the first to believe, the first to say "yes" to God's plan, and her journey is a model for all who seek to follow God's call. Her humility, strength, and unwavering devotion have inspired generations of believers, her life a symbol of the love that overcomes all challenges.

Mary's legacy endures in the hearts of the faithful. She is revered not only as the mother of Jesus but as a mother to all who seek God's grace. Her example teaches us that faith requires courage, that love endures even the greatest sorrows, and that God's promises are true. Her story invites believers to walk with hope, to embrace God's plan, and to trust that, even in the face of suffering, God's love is always present.

Mary's role in the early Church and her legacy as a model of faith continue to guide and inspire. She is remembered as a figure of strength, compassion, and holiness, her life a beacon of light for all who seek to know God more deeply. Through her example, we are reminded that faith is not merely a belief but a journey, a path walked with humility, love, and the quiet strength that comes from a heart open to God.

Reflection on Mary's Legacy of Faith

Mary's life offers a profound message of hope and faith for every believer. From her acceptance of God's will to her presence at the cross, she demonstrated that true faith embraces both joy and sorrow, both promise and sacrifice. Her journey is a testament to the power of love and the strength of a heart wholly devoted to God.

In Mary, we see a model of discipleship, a life that reflects the grace and beauty of a soul aligned with God's purpose. Her legacy lives on in the Church, her faith a source of inspiration for all who seek to walk with God. Through Mary's story, we are reminded that God's love is greater than any fear, that His promises endure through all trials, and that a life lived in faith is a life that shines with the light of His presence.

Works Cited

The Bible. World English Bible. Public Domain, .

Protoevangelium of James. In The Apocryphal New Testament, translated by J. K. Elliott, Oxford University Press, 1993.

Gospel of Pseudo-Matthew. In The Other Gospels: Accounts of Jesus from Outside the New Testament, edited by Bart D. Ehrman and Zlatko Pleše, Oxford University Press, 2014.

Gospel of Mary. In The Nag Hammadi Scriptures, edited by Marvin Meyer, HarperOne, 2007.

CHAPTER 8: MARY AS A SPIRITUAL ICON AND HER INFLUENCE ACROSS GENERATIONS

The Rise of Mary as a Symbol of Faith in the Early Church

As the early Christian Church grew and spread across regions, Mary's life and faith continued to serve as a powerful model for believers. She was more than the mother of Jesus; she embodied the essence of discipleship and the willingness to say "yes" to God's will, even when faced with suffering and uncertainty. The early Church held Mary in profound reverence, seeing her as the first disciple, the first to trust in Jesus' mission and to embrace God's mystery.

The Gospel of Mary, a Gnostic text, reveals that women held a unique place within the early Christian community, often guiding and encouraging the apostles with insights born from a deep spiritual understanding. In Mary's life, early Christians found a foundation for their own struggles, a reminder that true discipleship calls for both faith and courage. Her strength at the cross, her unwavering belief, and her support for the apostles made her a figure of inspiration as they faced persecution and hardships.

Mary's presence became a spiritual anchor for early Christians, many of whom turned to her as an intercessor and a motherly figure who could understand their trials and joys. Her role as theotokos, or "God-bearer," emphasized her special connection to God and Jesus, establishing her as a bridge between heaven and earth. Believers found comfort in praying to Mary, asking for her guidance and intercession, as they sought to follow in her footsteps of humility and devotion.

Mary as the First and Greatest Disciple

Mary's example as the first disciple established a model of faith that inspired generations of believers. She exemplified what it meant to trust in God fully, her life a series of "yeses" to His will, from the Annunciation to the cross. Her unwavering faith at each pivotal moment—when Gabriel announced her role in God's plan, at Jesus' birth, during his ministry, and in the early Church—revealed a heart entirely open to God's purpose.

The Protoevangelium of James portrays Mary's life as one marked by purity and devotion, emphasizing her unique relationship with God even before she became the mother of Jesus. Her consecration in the Temple as a young girl, as recounted in this apocryphal text, symbolized her special role as a vessel for God's work. Early believers saw in Mary an unparalleled example of purity, selflessness, and steadfastness, qualities they sought to embody in their own lives.

Mary's response to God's call—her quiet acceptance, her steadfast support of Jesus, and her strength in times of sorrow—established her as the ultimate model of discipleship. She did not seek recognition or power; rather, her life was one of humble service, a path that resonated deeply with early Christians. Mary's life was a profound example of how one's faith could transform the world, not through public accolades but through quiet obedience to God's will.

Mary as an Intercessor and Symbol of Compassion

In the years following her Assumption, Mary's role as an intercessor became central to Christian devotion. Believers viewed her as a compassionate figure who, having lived through suffering, understood human pain and joy alike. Many apocryphal texts emphasize her maternal love and her role as a protector of the faithful. The Gospel of Pseudo-Matthew depicts her as a woman of deep empathy, a presence of warmth and support for the early Christian community.

Mary's title as "Mother of the Church" grew from this role of intercession. Believers found comfort in the idea that she continued to pray for them, to offer them guidance, and to carry their petitions to God. Her maternal compassion and her unshakable faith made her an enduring symbol of hope for those facing persecution and hardship. Her life, marked by both joy and sorrow, made her a relatable and accessible figure, a symbol of the Church's unity and endurance.

Through her example, believers found strength in their own journeys of faith. They prayed to Mary for comfort, healing, and guidance, seeing in her a mother who would never abandon them. She became a symbol of compassion, reminding them that they, too, could endure life's trials with grace and faith.

The Development of Marian Devotion and the Creation of Early Hymns and Prayers

As Christianity spread, so did devotion to Mary. Early hymns and prayers dedicated to her emerged, each one honoring her faith and purity. These devotions emphasized her role as a spiritual mother, intercessor, and guide. In churches across the early

Christian world, believers sang hymns that celebrated her life and called upon her to intercede for them, recognizing her as the compassionate mother who bridged the gap between humanity and the divine.

One early Christian hymn that remains popular today, the Ave Maria, reflects this devotion. The hymn expresses Mary's special status as "full of grace," a woman chosen by God for her purity and faith. Such hymns not only celebrated her life but also served as a means for believers to draw closer to her, to seek her guidance, and to feel her presence in their lives.

The tradition of Marian devotion spread rapidly, and Mary's life inspired the creation of countless prayers, hymns, and liturgies. Through these devotions, believers found a way to connect with Mary, to seek her intercession, and to remember the love that had defined her life. In every prayer, they honored the courage and humility that had led her to embrace God's call, a reminder that she remained present with them, lifting them up to God in her prayers.

Mary's Symbolic Role in Christian Theology: Theotokos and the New Eve

In Christian theology, Mary's significance was deepened through the title of Theotokos, or "God-bearer," a term that underscored her role as the mother of Jesus, who was both fully human and fully divine. The title, formalized at the Council of Ephesus in 431 AD, emphasized Mary's unique role in salvation history, affirming her as the woman chosen to bring God into the world. Through her, God's love and grace became incarnate, uniting heaven and earth in the person of Jesus.

Mary was also often referred to as the "New Eve," a title that drew a parallel between her obedience and Eve's disobedience in the

Garden of Eden. While Eve's actions led to the fall of humanity, Mary's faithful "yes" to God's plan made her a partner in humanity's redemption. This theological symbolism highlighted Mary's pivotal role in God's plan and established her as a figure of hope, reminding believers that obedience to God could restore what had been lost.

Through these titles, Mary became more than a historical figure; she was elevated to a symbol of Christian faith itself. The early Church saw her as a bridge to God, the compassionate mother who represented humanity's restored relationship with God. Her titles and theological symbolism became central to Christian devotion, shaping how believers understood their own relationship with the divine.

The Enduring Legacy of Mary: A Guide for All Generations

Mary's legacy endures as a source of strength and inspiration for believers of all generations. Her life reminds us that true faith requires courage, humility, and a heart open to God's will. She teaches us that discipleship means embracing both joy and suffering, trusting that God's promises will be fulfilled, even when the path is unclear.

Throughout the centuries, countless saints, theologians, and ordinary believers have turned to Mary as a model of faith. Her quiet strength, her unwavering love, and her deep connection to God resonate across time, inspiring believers to walk in her footsteps. Her life, both simple and profound, offers a blueprint for a life of devotion, one that brings us closer to God through humility and love.

Mary's presence lives on in the prayers, hymns, and teachings of the Church. She is a beacon of hope, a mother to all who seek God's grace, and a reminder that faith is a journey marked by trust, sacrifice, and the promise of eternal life. Her legacy calls us to follow her example, to say "yes" to God's call, and to embrace a life lived in faith.

Reflection on Mary's Universal Appeal

Mary's life, from her humble beginnings in Nazareth to her role as a spiritual icon, speaks to the universal human experience. She is a mother, a disciple, a guide, and a friend. Her story is one of love, courage, and a deep trust in God's purpose, qualities that transcend time and place. Whether in times of joy or sorrow, believers turn to Mary, finding in her a figure who understands, comforts, and inspires.

Through Mary, we see the beauty of a life lived in full surrender to God. Her journey reminds us that faith is not always easy but that it is always rewarding. Her presence invites us to deepen our own faith, to walk with courage, and to find strength in the love that connects us all. Mary's legacy continues to shine, a testament to the power of faith and the grace that flows from a life devoted to God.

Works Cited

The Bible. World English Bible. Public Domain, .

Protoevangelium of James. In The Apocryphal New Testament, translated by J. K. Elliott, Oxford University Press, 1993.

Gospel of Pseudo-Matthew. In The Other Gospels: Accounts of Jesus from Outside the New Testament, edited by Bart D. Ehrman and Zlatko Pleše, Oxford University Press, 2014.

Gospel of Mary. In The Nag Hammadi Scriptures, edited by Marvin Meyer, HarperOne, 2007.

CHAPTER 9: THE INFLUENCE OF MARIAN DEVOTION IN EARLY CHRISTIANITY AND BEYOND

The Early Christian Veneration of Mary

From the earliest days of the Church, Mary's life of devotion and faith held a special place within Christian worship and theology. Believers saw in her an example of steadfastness and humility, a life dedicated to God's will and love. This reverence began during Mary's lifetime, with the disciples and other followers looking to her as a source of strength and wisdom. After her Assumption, Mary became an enduring figure of devotion, her life celebrated in prayers, hymns, and sacred art.

In the early Church, Mary's presence represented the intimate relationship between humanity and God. Her life was a reminder of God's closeness to His people and His willingness to dwell among them. Mary became known as the Mother of the Church, a title that recognized her role in guiding and interceding for believers. The early Christians revered her not only as the mother of Jesus but as a mother to all who sought God's love and guidance.

The Protoevangelium of James emphasizes Mary's unique purity and her consecration from a young age, making her an example of holiness. Her role as theotokos, or "God-bearer," emphasized her special connection to Jesus and affirmed her role in God's salvation plan. Early Christians found in Mary a model of complete devotion, one who willingly sacrificed and suffered to bring God's love into the world.

The Spread of Marian Devotion and the Formation of Prayers and Liturgies

As Christianity spread, devotion to Mary blossomed. Her life and example inspired prayers, hymns, and liturgies dedicated to her honor. These devotions became a central aspect of worship, offering believers a way to connect with Mary's compassionate presence and her intercessory power. One of the earliest recorded prayers to Mary, the Sub Tuum Praesidium, or Under Your Protection, captures the essence of this early devotion:

"Under your protection we seek refuge, Holy Mother of God. Despise not our petitions in our necessities, but deliver us always from all dangers, O glorious and blessed Virgin."

This prayer, dating back to the third century, reflects Mary's role as a protector and guide. Believers sought her intercession in times of need, viewing her as a compassionate advocate who could bring their prayers to God. Her life of humility and faith served as a reminder of the love and strength that came from living in union with God.

In the Gospel of Mary, Mary is shown as a wise and respected leader, and this text emphasizes her unique insight into Jesus' teachings. Early Christian communities found in her an example of a spiritual leader who could bridge the gap between Jesus' earthly ministry and their own lives. Mary's insights into God's mysteries, her unwavering love, and her ability to comfort and guide the disciples became a foundation for Marian devotion.

The Influence of Marian Art and Symbolism in Early Christianity

Art became a powerful means of expressing Marian devotion. Early Christian art often depicted Mary as theotokos, the mother of Jesus, holding him in her arms. This image, tender and full of compassion, symbolized the love that bound them and the salvation that Christ brought to the world. Through these depictions, believers saw Mary not only as a mother but as a figure of divine grace, embodying God's love and compassion.

One of the earliest icons of Mary, known as the "Hodegetria" or "She Who Shows the Way," depicts her holding Jesus and pointing toward him as the path to salvation. This icon became a beloved image in the early Church, symbolizing Mary's role in guiding believers toward Christ. She was not the destination but the one who directed all toward her son, embodying the humility and selflessness that characterized her life.

The Gospel of Pseudo-Matthew and other apocryphal texts often emphasize Mary's compassion and her ability to bring comfort to those around her. Through art, early Christians could visualize her presence, her eyes often gazing tenderly upon those who prayed before her image. Mary's icons became a source of solace for believers, allowing them to feel close to her presence and to be reminded of her role as an intercessor.

Mary's Role in Early Christian Theology and the Title of "New Eve"

In addition to her role as theotokos, Mary came to be viewed as the "New Eve," a theological title that placed her in contrast to Eve in the Garden of Eden. Whereas Eve's actions had led to humanity's fall, Mary's obedience and faith led to the redemption of humanity through Jesus Christ. Early theologians such as Justin Martyr and

Irenaeus explored this symbolism, recognizing Mary as a pivotal figure in God's plan of salvation.

By accepting God's will at the Annunciation, Mary undid the disobedience of Eve, becoming a symbol of hope and restoration. Her role as the New Eve illustrated the belief that God's love could heal and transform even the deepest wounds. Through Mary, humanity found a new beginning, one rooted in faith, obedience, and a return to God's grace.

Mary's role as the New Eve also reinforced the Church's teachings on redemption, reminding believers that God's love and mercy were boundless. Her life served as a bridge between the Old and New Covenants, her "yes" to God marking the beginning of a new chapter in humanity's relationship with the divine. Mary's obedience, contrasted with Eve's disobedience, became a cornerstone of Christian theology, emphasizing the transformative power of faith.

The Continuity of Marian Devotion Across the Centuries

As Christianity spread through the Roman Empire and beyond, devotion to Mary only deepened. Saints, theologians, and mystics across centuries looked to Mary as a model of faith, drawing inspiration from her life. Her example became a central part of Christian spirituality, reminding believers of the value of humility, love, and a heart open to God's call.

The Protoevangelium of James and Gospel of Mary helped shape an understanding of Mary as a wise and compassionate figure, whose faith offered a path to closeness with God. Devotion to Mary expanded into various forms, including rosary prayers, Marian hymns, and celebrations such as the Feast of the Assumption. Each devotion reflected a different aspect of her life, her virtues, and her role as a guide for all who sought to walk in faith.

Mary's influence spread beyond the Church, her image embraced by cultures and societies who saw in her a symbol of compassion and strength. Her legacy became a source of comfort for those in need, a beacon for those in despair, and a reminder that God's love could bring healing to all who sought it.

Mary's Influence in Personal and Communal Prayer

Mary's example has inspired countless believers to approach God with humility and devotion. Her life is a model of quiet strength, teaching us that prayer is not only a practice of words but a way of life. Mary's "yes" to God at the Annunciation was the beginning of a lifelong prayer, a heart open to God's will and a life that reflected His love.

In personal and communal prayer, believers have found in Mary a source of intercession, asking her to pray on their behalf and to bring their petitions before God. Her compassion, symbolized in art and hymns, serves as a reminder that even the smallest acts of faith can bring us closer to God. In her life, Christians find the example of a prayer that does not seek for itself but surrenders to God's purpose, trusting that He will bring good from every trial.

Mary's influence on prayer has shaped the spirituality of countless individuals, teaching them to approach God with a heart that listens, trusts, and loves. Her life shows us that true prayer is not about asking but about being open to God's work within us, willing to walk wherever He calls, knowing that His love is always with us.

Reflection on Mary's Universal Legacy

Mary's life and devotion remain an eternal testament to faith that endures through all trials. She is a mother to the Church, a guide to all who seek God, and a reminder of the love that transcends time. Her example calls us to embrace faith with courage and to approach God with a heart open to His will.

Her influence reaches beyond religion, touching the hearts of all who seek compassion, strength, and hope. In Mary, we see the beauty of a life lived for others, a journey marked by trust and love. Her story is one that speaks to the universal human experience, reminding us that God's love is present in every moment, every trial, and every act of faith.

Mary's legacy invites us to walk in her footsteps, to carry her faith in our own lives, and to be vessels of God's love in the world. She teaches us that true devotion is not found in words but in a life that reflects God's grace. Her life remains a beacon for all who seek to know God, a testament to the power of faith that endures through all things.

Works Cited

The Bible. World English Bible. Public Domain, .

Protoevangelium of James. In The Apocryphal New Testament, translated by J. K. Elliott, Oxford University Press, 1993.

Gospel of Pseudo-Matthew. In The Other Gospels: Accounts of Jesus from Outside the New Testament, edited by Bart D. Ehrman and Zlatko Pleše, Oxford University Press, 2014.

Gospel of Mary. In The Nag Hammadi Scriptures, edited by Marvin Meyer, HarperOne, 2007.

CHAPTER 10:
MARY'S INFLUENCE
IN CHRISTIAN ART
AND LITERATURE
ACROSS THE AGES

Early Christian Art and Symbolism of Mary

I n the first centuries of Christianity, Mary was depicted with profound reverence, yet artistic portrayals remained modest due to the early Church's cautious approach to iconography. Early Christian symbols, like the fish, cross, and anchor, conveyed faith in secret due to persecution, but Mary's presence appeared subtly in catacomb paintings and frescoes in places like Rome. In one of the earliest known Marian images from the Priscilla Catacombs, dating back to the second century, Mary is shown as a veiled figure holding the infant Jesus, symbolizing her role as the God-bearer, or theotokosuncil of Ephesus in 431 AD, which formally recognized Mary as theotokos, catalyzed a wave of Marian art. This title, meaning "Mother of God," emphasized her pivotal role in salvation, and art began to reflect this theological elevation. Artists in the Byzantine Empire depicted Mary in icons, often enthroned with the Christ child, and frequently surrounded by gold backgrounds symbolizing heaven. The Byzantine icon known as the "Hodegetria," or "She Who Shows the Way," depicts Mary pointing to Jesus as the path to salvation, reinforcing her role as intercessor and spiritual guide for believers .

le Ages: Mary as the Queen of Heaven and Mother of Mercy**

During the Middle Ages, Marian devotion flourished, and her image became prominent in Gothic cathedrals across Europe. Gothic art celebrated Mary as Queen of Heaven, depicting her crowned and often surrounded by angels. Cathedrals, like Notre Dame in Paris, are architectural homages to Mary, adorned with sculptures, stained glass, and rose windows that illustrate scenes from her life, her Assumption, and her role as an intercessor. The Notre Dame name, meaning "Our Lady," reflects the dedication of these grand structures to Mary .

In literature, fluence emerged in medieval hymns and poems. The "Ave Maria," inspired by Gabriel's greeting, became a central part of Christian liturgy. St. Bernard of Clairvaux's sermons in the 12th century praised Mary as the compassionate mother of mercy, establishing her as a mediator between humanity and God. This perception grew in Dante Alighieri's Divine Comedy, where Mary is depicted as the compassionate intercessor guiding Dante's soul to salvation. She is represented as the ultimate embodiment of divine grace, reflecting the medieval Church's view of her as a heavenly advocate .

Renaissance Art: Mary's Devotion and Grace

The Renaissance marked a shift in Marian art, emphasizing humanized, intimate portrayals. Artists like Leonardo da Vinci, Michelangelo, and Raphael depicted Mary as a compassionate mother, focusing on her gentle love for the Christ child. In Raphael's "Madonna and Child" series, Mary is portrayed with tenderness, emphasizing her maternal love and purity. Michelangelo's "Pietà," a sculpture of Mary holding the lifeless body of Jesus, captures her sorrow and strength, underscoring her role in Christ's suffering and her own enduring faith .

Literature of the Renaissance, poetry and hymns, continued to honor Mary's role. Writers praised her virtues, viewing her as a model for female purity, humility, and obedience. This era established Mary as a figure of both divine and human qualities, embodying both heavenly grace and relatable maternal love.

Modern Art and Literature: Diverse Representations of Mary's Universal Appeal

In modern times, Marian art and literature reflect a wide range of interpretations. Mary has been depicted as a symbol of peace, unity, and justice. Salvador Dalí's surrealist painting "The Madonna of Port Ligate" explores Mary as a figure who bridges the spiritual and physical worlds, reflecting humanity's yearning for divine connection. Writers like Rainer Maria Rilke and Gerard Manley Hopkins have continued to explore Marian themes, focusing on her faith, humility, and universal love .

Through centuries of art and literature, ge has evolved, yet her core symbolism of compassion, grace, and spiritual guidance remains enduring and universal.

Works Cited

The Bible. World English Bible. Public Domain, .

de Blaauw, Sible. "Mary in Early Christian Art and Iconography." The Cult of the Virgin Mary in the Middle Ages: East and West, edited by Mary Clayton and Hugh Magennis, Cambridge University Press, 2008, pp. 11-37.

Elliott, J. K., translator. The Apocryphal New Testament: A Collection of Apocryphal Christian Literature in an English Translation. Oxford University Press, 1993.

Ehrman, Bart D., and Zlatko Pleše, editors. The Other Gospels: Accounts of Jesus from Outside the New Testament. Oxford University Press, 2014.

Meyer, Marvin, editor. The Nag Hammadi Scriptures: The International Edition. HarperOne, 2007.

Underhill, Evelyn. Mysticism in Art and Literature. Constable, 1911.

CHAPTER 11: MARY IN THE THEOLOGY OF DIFFERENT CHRISTIAN TRADITIONS

Eastern Orthodox Tradition: Mary as Theotokos and the Spiritual Mother

In Eastern Orthodoxy, Mary is primarily honored as theotokos, or "Mother of God." This title, confirmed at the Council of Ephesus, holds central theological importance, affirming the divine and human natures of Christ. Eastern Orthodox believers view Mary as the bridge between heaven and earth, a compassionate intercessor who is deeply revered in liturgy. Icons of Mary, such as the "Panagia" or "All-Holy," are venerated, and Orthodox prayers like the Akathist Hymn celebrate her as a protector and comforter .

The Orthodox Church teaches that Mary experienced ion—a peaceful falling asleep—before her Assumption, symbolizing her unique place in God's plan. In Orthodox theology, Mary is seen not only as a model of purity but also as a symbol of victory over death, embodying the hope of resurrection for all believers .

Catholic Tradition: Mary as the Immaculate Conceptioatrix

In Roman Catholicism, Mary is honored with multiple titles that emphasize her sinless nature and intercessory role. The doctrine of the Immaculate Conception, formally defined in 1854, teaches that Mary was conceived without original sin, preparing her to bear Christ. Catholics also revere Mary as Mediatrix, meaning she intercedes on behalf of believers, and as Co-Redemptrix, sharing in Jesus' redemptive suffering.

Marian dogmas such as the Assumption, recognized in 1950, hold that Mary was assumed body and soul into heaven. This belief highlights her role in salvation and reinforces her position as a heavenly advocate for humanity. Catholic devotions, including the Rosary, the Ave Maria, and the Salve Regina, reflect a deeply personal relationship with Mary as a motherly intercessor.

Protestant Tradition: Mary as a Model of Faith and Humility denominations generally focus on Mary as a model of humility and obedience, emphasizing her role as the mother of Jesus while avoiding the level of veneration seen in Catholic and Orthodox traditions. Reformers like Martin Luther and John Calvin acknowledged Mary's importance in salvation history, but they resisted doctrines like the Immaculate Conception and Assumption, emphasizing instead her faithfulness and example of discipleship.

Today, many Protestant communities regard Mary with respect as a symbol of obedience to God's will and as a woman of faith. Marian hymns and scripture readings during Advent highlight her role in the Incarnation, while keeping devotion focused primarily on Christ.

Works Cited

The Bible. World English Bible. Public Domain, .

Elliott, J. K., translator. The Apocryphal New Testament: A Collection of Apocryphal Christian Literature in an English Translation. Oxford University Press, 1993.

Ehrman, Bart D., and Zlatko Pleše, editors. The Other Gospels: Accounts of Jesus from Outside the New Testament. Oxford University Press, 2014.

Louth, Andrew. Introducing Eastern Orthodox Theology. InterVarsity Press, 2013.

Pelikan, Jaroslav. Mary Through the Centuries: Her Place in the History of Culture. Yale University Press, 1996.

Schreck, Alan. Catholic and Christian: An Explanation of Commonly Misunderstood Catholic Beliefs. Servant Books, 2004.

Meyer, Marvin, editor. The Nag Hammadi Scriptures: The International Edition. HarperOne, 2007.

CHAPTER 12: THE GLOBAL MARY: MARY'S INFLUENCE IN DIFFERENT CULTUREIONAL PRACTICES

Latin American Devotion: Our Lady of Guadalupe

In Latin America, Mary's appearance as Our Lady of Guadalupe in 1531 is one of the most profound expressions of Marian devotion. According to tradition, Mary appeared to an indigenous peasant, Juan Diego, in Mexico, requesting a church be built in her honor. Her image, miraculously imprinted on Juan Diego's cloak, features her wearing traditional Aztec symbols, embodying a connection between indigenous culture and Catholicism. Our Lady of Guadalupe is celebrated as a protector of the poor and a symbol of unity and justice .

European Marian Shrines: Lourdes and Fatima

In Europe, Marian apparitions in Lourdes, France, and Fatima, Portugal, have drawn millions of pilgrims seeking healing, peace, and spiritual renewal. In Lourdes, Mary appeared to Saint Bernadette in 1858, proclaiming herself the Immaculate Conception. The healing waters of Lourdes continue to attract pilgrims, affirming Mary's role as a compassionate mother who intercedes for the sick and suffering .

At Fatima, Mary appeared to three shepherd children in 1917, delivering messages of repentance and world peace. Devotion to Our Lady of Fatima is especially strong in Portugal and other Catholic communities, where her message of peace and conversion resonates with believers .

Asian Devotion: Our Lady of La Vang in Vietnam

In Vietnam, Our Lady of La Vang holds profound religious and cultural significance. During religious persecution in the late 18th century, Mary reportedly appeared to Vietnamese Catholics seeking refuge in the forest of La Vang. She encouraged them to persevere, promising protection. Devotion to Our Lady of La Vang symbolizes hope and endurance for Vietnamese Catholics, connecting Marian devotion with cultural identity and survival .

African Marian Devotion: Our Lady of Kibeho

In Rwanda, Our Lady of Kibeho appeared to young schoolgirls in warning of impending violence and urging repentance and prayer. These messages gained special significance during the Rwandan Genocide, when believers saw Mary's warnings as prophetic. The shrine of Our Lady of Kibeho has become a place of reconciliation, where pilgrims seek healing and unity.

Works Cited

The Bible. World English Bible. Public Domain, .

Elliott, J. K., translator. The Apocryphal New Testament: A Collection of Apocryphal Christian Literature in an English Translation. Oxford University Press, 1993.

Ehrman, Bart D., and Zlatko Pleše, editors. The Other Gospels: Accounts of Jesus from Outside the New Testament. Oxford University Press, 2014.

Gibson, David. The Rule of Benedict: Pope Benedict XVI and His Battle with the Modern World. HarperOne, 2006.

Pelikan, Jaroslav. Mary Through the Centuries: Her Place in the History of Culture. Yale University Press, 1996.

Sanchez, Joseph P. Our Lady of Guadalupe: Devotions, Traditions, and Celebrations. Liturgical Press, 2012.

Meyer, Marvin, editor. The Nag Hammadi Scriptures: The International Edition. HarperOne, 2007.

Conclusion: Mary, the Cornerstone of Christian Faith and a Timeless Model of Devotion

Mary, the mother of Jesus, remains one of Christianity's most revered figures, embodying the virtues of faith, humility, and unwavering devotion to God's will. Her journey, which began in the humble village of Nazareth, reflects a life touched by extraordinary faith, unparalleled grace, and a unique place in God's redemptive plan. From the Annunciation to her Assumption, Mary's life has become a testament to the power of saying "yes" to God—a decision that would shape not only her destiny but the course of human history.

Mary's journey begins with her acceptance of God's call, as narrated in the Gospel of Luke, when the angel Gabriel appears to her, announcing that she will bear the Son of God (Luke 1:26-38,

WEB). Her simple yet profound response, "Behold, the servant of the Lord; let it be done to me according to your word" (Luke 1:38, WEB), reflects an obedience that became the foundation for her role as theotokos, the "God-bearer." This defining moment in Christian history represents the ultimate act of faith and humility. The Protoevangelium of James, an apocryphal text, underscores Mary's purity and unique calling from an early age. It portrays her as consecrated and dedicated to God even before the Annunciation. Throughout Jesus' life, from his infancy to his ministry, Mary's role is depicted as pivotal and divinely ordained.

It also reveals a mother's enduring faith and resilience. She witnesses his first miracle at Cana, where her subtle intervention leads to the transformation of water into wine, symbolizing her belief in her son's divine mission (John 2:1-11, WEB). Mary's role at the crucifixion, where she stands at the foot of the cross, is a profound testament to her strength and sorrow as both mother and disciple. As foretold by Simeon, a "sword" pierces her soul (Luke 2:35, WEB), marking her as a figure of redemptive suffering. Her steadfast presence through Jesus' crucifixion solidifies her as a central figure in the narrative of salvation.

Mary's journey suffixion. According to the Gospel of Pseudo-Matthew and other early Christian traditions, her life continued among the apostles, guiding and encouraging them as they established the early Church. The Gospel of Mary further emphasizes her spiritual insight and leadership among the disciples, particularly in moments of uncertainty. Early Christian communities saw her as a symbol of unwavering faith and the first true disciple of Christ. This role as both mother and follower solidifies Mary as a cornerstone of the Christian faith and an intercessor for believers, embodying the Church's unity and resilience.

Mary's enduring influence is seen in theology and global devotion, reflecting her universal appeal across cultures and denominations. From Byzantine icons like the "Hodegetria" to

Renaissance masterpieces by Michelangelo and Raphael, artists have depicted Mary with reverence, emphasizing both her divine connection and human compassion. Marian hymns, prayers such as the **Ave Maria**, and centuries-old traditions like the Rosary have drawn believers closer to her, connecting them to her example of faith and obedience. Her titles, such as "Mother of Mercy," "Queen of Heaven," and "Our Lady," highlight her multifaceted role as a compassionate mother, an intercessor, and a symbol of divine grace..

Each Christian tradition holds Mary in unique regard, God's will. The Orthodox Church venerates her as theotokos and celebrates her Dormition, viewing her as a bridge between heaven and earth. In Catholicism, Mary is revered as the Immaculate Conception and Assumed into Heaven, roles that underscore her purity and unique relationship with Christ. Protestantism, while cautious of Marian veneration, honors her as a model of faith and humility, particularly during Advent and Christmas. These varying perspectives reflect Mary's adaptability and her continued relevance within Christian theology, uniting believers across denominations .

The influence of Mary transcends cultural and geographic boundaries, manifesting in wide. In Latin America, she appears as Our Lady of Guadalupe, an icon of hope and justice for the marginalized. In Europe, Marian shrines like Lourdes and Fatima have become places of pilgrimage, healing, and spiritual renewal. In Vietnam, Our Lady of La Vang represents resilience for a people who have faced persecution, while in Rwanda, Our Lady of Kibeho calls for reconciliation and peace. These global devotions underscore Mary's role as a symbol of compassion, unity, and endurance for people of diverse backgrounds and cultures .

Mary's life and legacy serve as a universal call to faith, obedience, and love. She is a mother, a disciple, and a guiding presence. Her journey, marked by humility, strength, and a profound trust in God, remains a model for every believer. Mary's example shows that true faith endures through joy and sorrow, that love transcends all trials, and that God's grace is always present for those who trust in His plan. She is the cornerstone of the Church's faith, a living testament to the beauty of a life surrendered to God.

As Christianity continues to evolve, Mary's legacy remains timeless, inspiring countless generations to live with courage, compassion, and devotion. Her life calls believers to walk with God, to say "yes" to His will, and to trust in the promise of salvation. Through Mary, the Church finds a mother who understands, a disciple who leads by example, and a bridge that connects heaven and earth. Her story is a reminder that faith is not only a path to God but a journey walked in love, bringing God's light into the world.

Works Cited

The Bible. World English Bible. Public Domain, .

Protoevangelium of James. In The Apocryphal New Testament, translated by J. K. Elliott, Oxford University Press, 1993.

Gospel of Pseudo-Matthew. In The Other Gospels: Accounts of Jesus from Outside the New Testament, edited by Bart D. Ehrman and Zlatko Pleše, Oxford University Press, 2014.

Gospel of Mary. In The Nag Hammadi Scriptures, edited by Marvin Meyer, HarperOne, 2007.

de Blaauw, Sible. "Mary in Early Christian Art and Iconography." The Cult of the Virgin Mary in the Middle Ages: East and West, edited by Mary Clayton and Hugh Magennis, Cambridge University Press, 2008, pp. 11-37.

Pelikan, Jaroslav. Mary Through the Centuries: Her Place in the History of Culture. Yale University Press, 1996.

THE END

Made in the USA
Las Vegas, NV
29 December 2024

15564721R00039